Choose a simple living
- Your life is as you choose to live it

An emotional- and thought-provoking book that gives insight into choosing a simple live, which can give an overview and peace. The book requires presence, and in this presence, I experienced a deep inner peace and distant healing. The book provides more than just technical knowledge. At the end of each section the reader is encouraged to immerse itself in the issues in relation to one's own life. This inspired me to reflect on the issues after having laid down the book. The book can be used as a reference book, since each section is completed. The book enters spiritual as well as more mundane topics. The contents can be used as concrete tools that I have started to use in my everyday life. If you would like to have concrete explanations on that there is more to life than the obvious, *Choose a Simple Living*, is a comprehensive book.

- *Rikke Jehs Løh*, teaches Mindfulness & yoga.

Choose a simple living
- Your life is as you choose to live it

by Erik Istrup

Choose a simple living
- Your life is as you choose to live it

Copyright © 2013 Erik Istrup

Publisher: Erik Istrup Publishing © 2013

Print & distribution: Ingram Spark

Typeface: Palatino

ISBN: 978-87-994659-9-6

Genre: Body, Mind & Spirit

Erik Istrup Publishing
Igimaq 8, 3905 Nuussuaq, Greenland
www.erikistrup.dk/publishing/

Index

Prelude

Thousands of books have been written in many languages about self-development, so what does this book tell you the others do not? Nothing! It says nothing that has not already been said; it has the same message that has always been brought to humanity, but because we are all different and require different ways of learning, this book was created. Books that were written many years ago, written in another time, in another consciousness and for people with a different understanding than the people living today will not work these days. What was written at that time was the truth that was needed at the time. The truth presented today fits today's awareness that can hold so much more information than was previously possible. It can be compared with two sponges: the 2000-year-old sponge can contain one pint of water, while the sponge today, can contain 10 pints. Here symbolises water truth.

Many books about personal development start by explaining how to drop everything we have picked up in our lives until now. Usually, there is a lot that we would like to discard, and it can seem quite overwhelming. I choose to start with the foetus and go the other way. When we understand why we are who we are and live as we do, it will be easier to get rid of the things that we no longer want to be a part of ourselves. Before we focus on the embryo and human development, there are some concepts that we have to review.

With the title *Choose a Simple Living* I urge you to choose to live your life based on simple principles instead of choosing to make life complicated and confusing. While writing this book I focused on making the message simple. If trying to explain too much, the message often becomes complex and, therefore, more difficult to understand and use in daily life. When something is complex, the mind begins to think too much and seek solutions and possible problems with these solutions. Thinking can therefore create more problems than it solves. Here you must feel if the message rings true for you. You may sometimes feel that what I say is somewhat vague, but it is difficult to give concrete examples which everyone can use because we indeed are different. By keeping the explanations on a more general level, the information is relevant to all who read them. You must then try to see how you can best use them. For simplicity, I will paint you a picture with few colours, and not too many shades, and then it is up to you to continue the painting. And, as always, you must use your common sense and take from this book what is relevant to your own life. When you read the book, it might feel somewhat sterile at times. I have intentionally not added much of myself, but have had a focus on bringing you information and guidance. Now and then I come forward between the lines, and we meet "face to face". If we disregard the offset in time, we can say that I'm sitting at my computer writing to you while you're reading it. We can therefore meet in this common "now" if we imagine that we are sitting "on each side of the paper".

Each chapter ends with some additional questions or comments. This allows you to choose to go deeper into yourself, as a kind of deeper awareness work that can help you further on the way. It may look as if some of the points are equal in their content, but as you know, an incomprehensible question can be understandable if it is simply presented in different words. Many of the points are questioning the way you live and think or, more precisely, what you, as a person, are doing. You might find that you meet opposition against working with the points: you can't be bothered, you are too tired, you do not understand the points or you feel a sudden anger directed towards them and so on. It is a very natural response. It is the "person" part of you that is fighting for its life. It feels that you are attempting to undermine its importance in your life. And it is right. You, therefore, need to make it clear that it is a natural part of your life when it comes to interaction with other people, and that you simply relieve it from some of its work. All this may sound somewhat incomprehensible, but I will elaborate on it later. Here I will only prepare you for what you may experience, and at the same time, tell you that it is okay if you have such experiences.

There are some words marked with an asterisk (*) the first time it occurs in the text. These are explained in the glossary section.

Thanks

I would like to thank all who have encouraged me in my work to complete the vague thoughts that started this release, and those who have read early drafts and given suggestions, especially Lenna Lisbeth Nønne Rasmussen and Natalie Key, who have read multiple versions and provided valuable comments and suggestions on how I could improve the content and make it more accessible.

Glossary

3D: Three-dimensional. On Earth, we have three dimensions: length, width and height. Some see time as a dimension. I see time as being an attribute of 3D, so that we can experience a sense of past, present and future.

Aspect: part of. For example, we can say that the soul is an aspect of All That Is.

DNA (from http://en.wikipedia.org/wiki/DNA): deoxyribonucleic acid (DNA) is a molecule that encodes the genetic instructions used in the development and functioning of all known living organisms and many viruses.

Double slit experiment, the: Physics proves that the observer exists and that our world exists only because of the observer. Very short: Electrons behave as "wave energy" when they are not observed/measured, but as particles, i.e. solid, when they are observed/measured. It is therefore, the observer or the consciousness that makes the "invisible" waves become visible substance. See also the chapter References.

Duality: Divided into two parts; something composed of two parts; that there are contradictions.

Energy information: e.g. a cup consists of energy, and energy contains at the same time information like properties of shape, colours, materials and so on. Non-physical things contain information about other properties.

Bevel: Perspective, e.g. a bevel-sanded diamond: the world looks different, depending on the surface of the diamond you choose to see it through, but it is still the same world you are looking at.

Mantra: one or more words, or a phrase that continually repeats, or as meditation, in order to keep the focus on the present moment and calming thoughts and emotions.

Down-transform: when you put a chain of lights on the Christmas tree, a transformer is sitting on the chord turning the voltage in the socket from 110 or 230 volts to 12 volts. It is also what has happened when you wake up after a dream: what your higher consciousness experiences while you slept you are down-transforming into your human consciousness and dreams "come out" containing less than the original experiences, when presented to the three-dimensional awareness.

Neuropeptide (NPY) (from http://en.wikipedia. org/wiki/NPY): an organic chemical compound, consisting of small chains of amino acids linked by peptide bonds.

Receptor: a receiving point on the surface of a cell that is coded to only receive substances with a specific structure or key where the receptor then locks.

I am talking to you

I choose to speak directly to you in what I write to get a closer contact and involve you personally so you do not believe it is "the others" I am talking to. Yes, I will be personal, and I hope that you choose to take it in as practical tools for use in your life. I say nothing to offend or demean you; I will provoke you, yes, but only to make you aware of something and maybe get you to think differently and consider making and seeing things in new ways. It is all about growth. If you are dissatisfied with what we have, or are, you must take responsibility for transforming the situation. By thinking differently and doing things in a new way, life will change as well, since a new direction will lead you to new possibilities.

Everything I present for you is presented with the greatest love and respect. Therefore, it is always a good idea to ask about the feelings that emerge when you read the book, since it would get you to discover new things about yourself. Know that they belong to you.

Self-development

Self-development means that your self-conscious chooses to develop. The self is the conscious part of you. I will get into more details later. It is the will to do it that sets the process in motion. This also applies in cases where a person "throws in the towel" because he or she no longer bothers to be in their present position or find a solution to this. We surrender. In reality, it means "I give up", giving themselves over to all available potentials and not just keep living with their present believe.

Later, when you look back at when your self-development began to take flight, you may discover that there were some things that you would say were not conscious choices on your part. I will later show you that each of us creates our own lives, which means that the initial events are also created by you, but on a deeper level than your daily thinking and current awareness.

Self-development is very much about getting a recognition of what you are a part of. It is about getting an overview and seeing a consistency in your life. This overview removes the frustration of not being able to understand your own situation. When this frustration disappears, you get a larger surplus in life. Overview gives a surplus.

Self-development is also self-insight. It requires

that you look "inwards" and discover that you contain much more than you were first aware of. You get a better picture of what you are and, not least, what you are not. This means that you must accept that this is you, no matter you consider it good or bad. After the acceptance, you can choose what to keep, but we discuss this later. There is nothing that is good or bad, but that is how we tend to judge both the world and ourselves.

For thorough study

- Under what circumstances did you become aware of this book?

- Do you see it as a coincidence that you came across this book, or do you feel that it was intended that you should discover it?

- Is there an event that has started your conscious development, and were there some small signs that led up to this event?

- How will you define self-development?

- Are there one or more goals in your life and, if there are, how do you define these goals?

- How do you see yourself in relation to these objectives?

- Where can the objectives of self-development

and goals in life come from?

The truth

We may also use the term "layers of truth". Imagine that truth is structured in layers. The basic truth is at the bottom and describes very simply how everything is connected. This does not mean that the truth becomes more complex the higher you go up in the stack of layers. Something is only truth when understood and when something is understood it becomes single. I am thinking not so much of the mental understanding, but more about the awareness that something is the truth.

The truth that you encounter will always be only a part of the truth. If you compare two truths, they can initially be contradictory, but with a third (and higher) truth, the first two are seen as valid facets* of a larger whole. You are, therefore, not necessarily up against having to choose between two statements, where only one is "the truth".

A banal example might be that you speak with two of your friends, and you mention a person who is not present and say that he is German. One of your friends says, convincingly, that he is Italian; he has even heard him speak fluent Italian. You are persistent in saying that he is German, for you were with him when he told some Germans, in perfect German, how they could find the hotel they were looking for. The friend who has not yet spoken, can tell that the person was actually born and raised in Italy, just across the border from Germany. Here, the third person brings together the two immediate antagonists to a logical truth, namely that the person is bilingual and can, by reason of his birthplace, speak both languages fluently.

Therefore, when you read something that you feel you do not understand or that does not match anything you have previously read or heard, take it merely as information and a possible truth, for perhaps another truth is emerging alongside the previous information which makes it fall into place in a wider context. The greater truth is forced to come in small pieces, because it takes time to incorporate it into our current perception of the truth. It is even harder if you have to throw away some of the old, knowing that it has formed a foundation in your life, but which now can be replaced by a larger truth. The old truth can be so hard to get rid of that one chooses to deny the new truth that we have encountered and lives on with the old. An old truth may be that one is convinced that we must work eight hours a day; the work is hard and we are sick and tired when we come home. If you met a person who is only at work for four hours a day, loves to work and comes home energised, you will be inclined to think that the same cannot apply to you. However, this person has just shown you that it can be done; maybe it was why you met the person. Just as all people are equally worthy of having a good life, which is an assertion on my part, of course, it also applies to you. In this connection, an old truth for you may just be that you are not worthy of a good life. This truth may hinder you in even trying to pursue the truth of a four-hour working day, not to speak of four-hour work every week.

The old phrase "better the devil you know than the devil you don't" fits well into this idea of not daring to choose something else. It is fear of the unknown and fear of not being able to handle and live up to something bigger. One feels too small and insignificant, and cannot imagine oneself in a role that is more than what it is now. However, that is precisely what personal development is about.

This fear of something new is quite normal. It is a survival instinct that should prevent us from doing dangerous things. But, at the same time, you might just survive if you act differently than you normally would, and thereby discover new opportunities. These new opportunities can be a greater truth.

The truth comes to us not only as the spoken or written word, pictures and movies and other sensory impressions; in fact, we get more energy information* than "general" information. Energy information is data or the properties of someone or something that we encounter. You may look at a photo of a person, and you experience "knowing" something about this person, not shown in the picture. It can also be called consciousness-information, as you will be aware of something without actually having used your main senses to get hold of it. This can be expressed in a thought or an idea. With the term consciousness-information, I mean wisdom that flows to you from your higher self. Later, I will tell you more of the higher self, but you can see it as your inner core. Therefore, be aware that all events you experience and information that you receive, whatever their origin, can be something that you can use in your life. For example, the answer to a question that you have asked or a guiding principle toward a right answer.

Note that each human speaks his own truth from the experience they have had in life. This means that the person sees life through his glasses of experience, where the experiences are the basis for that person's perception of truth.

For thorough study

- Have you heard something that you certainly knew was wrong from the knowledge that you had but then later found out that what you had heard was also correct?

- How would you feel, if you know that every-thing you encountered wase the truth when you disregard the "ordinary lies" you experi-ence?

- Try to explain what the truth is for you. Give some examples.

- Do you know or can you remember where those truths come from?

Part 1: Consciousness

To be aware of one's consciousness

If the two of us were to meet and talk you may, at some point in the conversation, mention that you **have** a body and not that **are** your body. It is thus clear that you are **aware** that you have a body, but that it is not the whole you. Just the way you describe your body shows that you do not identify yourself with the body. For example, if you lose a leg, you lose something of the body well enough, but you do not feel the same way that you lose something of yourself, i.e. that there has been less of you.

When you talk about feelings, you might often say that "I feel…". You are here less conscious that you **have** feelings and not that you **are** the feelings.

The same applies to thoughts. You **are** thinking something more than you **have** thought.

These examples of body, feelings and thoughts that I have just mentioned suggest that you are aware that the body is a part of you, while you see thoughts and feelings as being you. It is what you want to say that you are; the person you are.

The consciousness that perceives the body, mind and feelings must necessarily be something else and be "located" somewhere else than those things in order to be able to observe them. I would call this observing awareness the observer. This term is also used in other contexts, and some may call it your soul.

The following drawing is a very simplified model that should not be considered the truth, but only serve as an illustration.

The human being

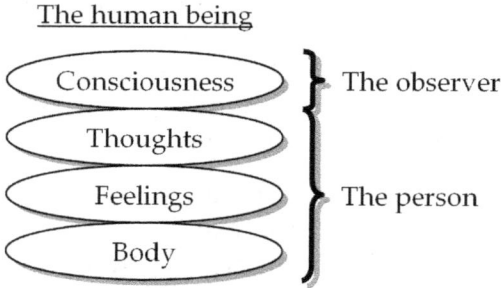

Your senses are mostly situated in your head. I am here thinking of the vision, hearing, taste and smell, so you might be inclined to believe that "you" are in the head. You are sensing with your body as well, so you are aware that you have a body. You can of course see it as well.

It is neither your thoughts nor your emotions that sense the world around you. "It is my brain," you might be inclined to respond. Consciousness is not brain thoughts; consciousness is what the mind is thinking. And where are the emotions situated?

After what I have just said, when I ask you about where your "I" "sits", which I do now, you may want to reply that "mind is in the brain and it is who I am". Now, I ask you where you think that emotions such as joy or hatred sit, and you may answer, perhaps by linking emotions and thoughts together, but you cannot really place it in the physical body, or outside it for that matter.

All this talk about the observer and the person is to show you that it is **you** that are the consciousness which is the observer, and that you have a human identity or personality and that you are not this person. It is just difficult to distinguish what is what because all this is so closely connected and works so perfectly together.

I remember that, as a child, I was wondering why exactly I looked through these eyes. Why did I not look out of a second pair of eyes and why was I placed in just this body? These considerations have meant that I, at any level, have always felt special because no one else ever talked about such a thing. It was also a hint for me that I was more than what could be seen. I did not act upon this truth, but certainly kept in mind that there is something "bigger" or at least something "more".

The first step for you to get the observer in focus,

is to divide thoughts and emotions as two separate concepts or features. By using "Vipasana" meditation technique (see the chapter on meditation), you will be aware that thoughts can calm down. You can **be** without thinking. The first time it happens is usually a great experience. It is about finding the calm within yourself. In the beginning, you might require silence around you. Later on, these sounds are just a part of the world and not you, and you will not be upset by them, just as you are not disturbed by thoughts and emotions.

When the mind chatter does not disturb you, you can be more aware of yourself, i.e. your real self. By just observing your feelings and still be conscious that you exist, then you are being aware that you are the observer, the "I" that is aware that it is aware without distracting thoughts and feelings. At this point, you are fully aware that the body is not your real "I", in the same way that the thoughts and feelings are not.

I have experienced that without disturbing thoughts and feelings, I had much more energy than before. I found out how much energy I had previously spent on unnecessary thoughts and emotions that wear one out. Perhaps I am obliged here to point out that you obviously have not become "brain-dead" and emotionally cold; you are just getting rid of all the "noise" that previously filled your life and took incredible amounts of energy that you could have used with what we call positive thoughts and feelings. You now have a surplus, both to yourself and to the people around you.

You can receive noise in the form of discomfort and pain from your body that will disturb you during meditation. They are signals that tell you there is something that brings disharmony in your life. You now have the possibility, in the silence of the meditation to inquire into what you can do to bring harmony back into your life. We will cover that later.

I have tried to get you to work you through each part of you and your human identity, body, thoughts and emotions, to give you a greater understanding of each part. The individual parts are working together, of course, and must therefore be seen both as independent functions and as a whole. I do this so you can see that there necessarily must be one or more "higher" yous. Now that you have "separated" yourself from thoughts and emotions, you can see these as tools in your life and in your interactions with the outside world.

Why did the observer choose to have a body and be here? Why can the observer not be here without all this attached? Well, you see, the body is a necessary tool for the observer, if it must sense, act, and react in this world of physical experience. The observer must be able to see themselves and others, create and express him- or herself; in short, live his or her life. Can the observer not live without the physical aspect*? Yes of course, but only by living in the physical, everything is much more intense. The analogy could be that you otherwise might just smell the food without being able to experience all the other facets of a meal. Just think of all the things that you could not do without a physical body in a physical world! I will elaborate on it later, but the observer wants to experience and grow through his experiences.

The observer also appears in your dreams: you've probably experienced that you have been in a dream where you realise that it is a dream. It is the observer who is aware that it is a dream. I will later get more into what dreams are and how they can be used.

Let us try to get a little more hold on what this observer is and where it originated. In the next section I will use the term "All That Is". It is the consciousness that is fully aware of itself. Are you ready? Then let us begin.

For thorough study

- Have you had experiences, which have shown you that you are the observer experiencing the person's thoughts and can you describe this experience?

- Have you had experiences, which have shown you that you are the observer experiencing the person's feelings and can you describe this experience?

- Have you experienced silence without thoughts and emotions and can you describe this experience?

- Do you remember the first time you experienced the feeling of being I AM and in what context?

Energy and consciousness

Consciousness cannot be fully explained since we are consciousness, but I will try to satisfy your intellect with the following description. All things are made of energy, but consciousness is not a thing and is not created by energy. Energy is, in short, a "non solid matter" used to build anything with physical substance. This is why we say that the physical world is an illusion. The energy appears here only in a manner that is perceived as solid.

When we talk about awareness, we can say that it is the catalyst or master builder who initiates a creation from focusing on some options out of endless possibilities.

It is, even so, that it is only the precursor to energy that is ready to be activated when an opportunity gets the focus of the consciousness. You can perhaps imagine that water drops are these dormant precursors. When awareness is focused on a possibility, all these water droplets are assembled into a lake which symbolises energy from wonderful ice sculptures can be created.

Consciousness has no extent, and therefore does not need room to exist. This means that space or extent is an illusion. If there is no space, there is no separation. Everything that is not consciousness does not exist for real. See the chapter "Dimensions".

Awareness does not use or "take" time and therefore does not exist in time. This means that time or a time period and what we know as the past, present and future is an illusion – see the chapter "Time".

At some point, I asked the following question to my higher self, "Can consciousness have its focus on something special and not on something else? If this is the case, we can speak of consciousness separation or sharing of consciousness."

It took months before I got a reply, "If you make a scale that goes from full consciousness to no consciousness, this scale can describe that one can be at different levels of consciousness. We can also describe it as a lens for a camera that can go from wide-angle, which corresponds to a large field of view and full consciousness to tele, equivalent to a small field of view and low awareness or consciousness."

"There is only one consciousness but since it is, so to speak, divided into smaller parts, as when we initially talked about All That Is, these consciousness parts have only a limited angle of consciousness, similar to the tele-lens. Place the full awareness of "All That Is" in the centre of a wheel, where the spokes represent parts of the whole consciousness and show that "All That Is's" awareness can "see" out of all the spokes at the same time."

I have mentioned earlier that thoughts are not the same as consciousness. Since it is consciousness that is the creative force, it is not the thought that in itself is creative. We may say that it is the idea or, really, the idea repeated many times that can induce a belief that becomes part of your life. The repeating idea serves as a mantra*. If you often think (from the feeling of not being good enough) that you are not good enough, you will eventually "create" this in your reality and see the coherence in your life. You "ask" for this to become your "reality". Because of this repetition, you actually hypnotise yourself to have this conviction.

For thorough study

- Can you find examples of repetitive thoughts or beliefs that appear in your life?

All That Is

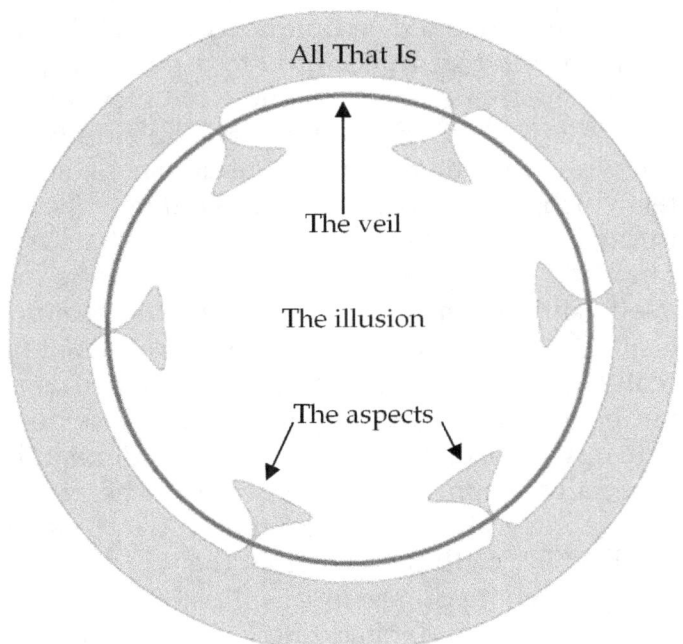

All That Is

The veil

The illusion

The aspects

"All That Is" and the illusion (simplified)

I will tell you a little story about why we are here. Before the universe was created the consciousness which we call "All That Is", was fully conscious of itself in its PURE BEING. All That Is got the idea that it would actively EXPERIENCE itself and not just be PASSIVE. How can one fully experience oneself if one knows everything about oneself? "All That Is" resolved this by creating aspects or parts of itself, each of which contained a unique combination of all it's properties. In addition to aspects forgetting where they came from and what they really are, "All That Is" created a place outside of it self with a curtain or veil of consciousness or filter which aspects could not immediately "see" through. It was the only opportunity that "All That Is", through the aspects, could experience itself without knowing itself. This playground is an illusion, because it does not show what is really happening. Because it is an illusion, it cannot be a part of "All That Is", but must be outside it. This is, of course, difficult to understand, especially when it is "All That Ss". Therefore, you can say about yourself that you "are also All That Is", with the view that the word "also" refers to what you are in this illusion. You will gain a greater understanding of this, when you read on.

When I talk about illusion, I mean that something is not what it appears to be. In this case, it is our three-dimensional world of more or less solid objects, i.e. "things" that are built of atoms.

As the researchers examined smaller and smaller parts of the atom, they found out that the atom is not built up of solid particles, but energy. When they investigated the energy, they found out that the components of this energy are infinite numbers of possibilities that first become substance when a consciousness starts a creation. (See the double-slit experiment* under the chapter "References".) By using one's imagination or fantasy and thereby enabling the possibilities it begins to attract energy, and the construction begins. In the case of a physical object, it is first formed on a non-physical level, after which it can be transformed* into frequencies to appear physically.

It sounds rather abstract, that the smallest building block is the opportunities, and the building master is consciousness. I would just mention that we cannot equate consciousness and thought, but would also wait to talk about the difference between these two concepts until later in the book.

I know that our physical brain cannot understand how opportunities can become solid, so here the brain must accept that there are things which it is not designed to understand. They are beyond its three-dimensional ability to comprehend. Thus, I have also said that the brain only works with an understanding of the three-dimensional world. Outside 3D, it is up to our consciousness to perceive or feel what it means in an intuitive way. We go from thinking to feeling, meaning sensing, and be more aware. This shows precisely that thoughts have its limitations.

I will conclude with the clarification by telling that the illusion is a safe place to experience, because it is simply not real. The body can take damage and die, but for "you", the observer, which is consciousness, it is safe.

If one of the above-mentioned aspects is able to see through the veil, it can see that individual aspects are not separate but part of "All That Is". This is a great experience of truth. When a human dies, its consciousness leaves through the veil, but retains its unique qualities and given experiences. The body's components are returned to the Earth.

"All That Is" may also have asked itself the first time it went into the illusion, "I wonder if I can recognise myself when I meet myself? Therefore, I can see "All That Is" in others and thereby myself." The desire is to experience and not just to be. When we humans want **to be** instead of **doing** it is just a deep-seated desire to be what we really are, namely "All That Is". "All That Is" is (or prior to the experience, was) pure being, but through us, the aspects; it is also doing or action.

For "All That Is" everything is very simple, namely, to experience. There are many facets and infinite possibilities here, so every second you are living, you do the will of "All That Is" (which is actually your own will), namely to experience whatever it is. In the "eyes" of "All That Is" there is no good or evil, just another facet of endless possibilities. "All That Is" cannot be harmed or killed. It is only from a limited human understanding that it looks that way. From this perspective, you are completely safe here. When I refer to "you", I mean the aspect of "All That Is" - the real you.

What answer will "All That Is" give, if you asked about the reasons why we are here?

1) I will experience all the facets of myself.

2) I will create and be creative.

3) I want to rediscover and recognise myself.

4) I want to feel all the emotions and experience the new ones.

If you can recognise some of these wishes as some you have expressed in relation to the fact that you have taken the first step to self-development, you have heard the voice of "All That Is" in yourself! Your own voice!

For thorough study

- Think about how the world would be if everyone had the knowledge of what "work" we really desire to do.

- Have you had experiences that point to the confirmation that you are an aspect of "All That Is"?

Can you see that the observer, from the previous chapter, fits very well with what I call an aspect of "All That Is"? I will give you a small story, seen from a slightly different angle. If you picture "All That Is" as a child with a child's immediate joy and simplicity, you might better be able to understand the feelings involved. The next story I will call "The love of All That Is".

The love of All That Is

Before the world was created, there was only "All That Is". Even in the infinite wisdom of "All That Is", it had only known itself "from the inside". Since "All That Is" was everything, and was not able to **experience** itself, but only to **be** itself; this consciousness decided to split itself into two, so it was able to "see" an aspect of itself. These two parts were not separate, but contained the male and the female aspects of "All That Is". The dividing into a masculine and a feminine part is, of course, very simplified, but it fits well as a three-dimensional understanding of the story. I choose deliberately not to use the terms male and female, as it easily brings associations to the male and female body. These two aspects, we can call them the king and the queen, fell in love with each other. This was actually a completely new feeling for "All That Is" and it was deliriously happy. The original feeling of love was the love of "All That Is" itself, a "selfish" love, but now the feeling of love had reached a new dimension. It had been more than it was before. "All That Is" has created something new! Although it was still about love for self, it was a love that, in one way or another, was turned outward. I know that the word selfish has a negative tone to many, but it is used here as quite neutral to describe love that is directed towards oneself.

"All That Is" wanted to experience more of this love, so in a way it was these two aspects, the queen and the king, who gave birth to some "children". To experience the ultimate love, "All That Is" created aspects of itself, princes and princesses, with a veil that prevented them from knowing "All That Is" and where they came from, their home, the first kingdom. Again, I will mention that the veil prevents aspects from knowing the full truth about what they are, namely "All That Is". Each of these aspects was born with a unique set of all qualities or attributes from the original father/mother. In addition to the opportunity to be able to experience the new feeling, love to another aspect of itself, now "All That Is" had the opportunity to experience all the other qualities of itself.

Eventually very much was experienced and at one point yet another type of love was experienced: unconditional love! Perhaps it is new to you, that the original love of "All That Is" was not unconditional love but "just" love for self. To find "All That Is" or the essence of "All That Is" in yourself, you must find the love for yourself.

As you can see from the story, "All That Is" has changed and will continue to change, depending on other experiences made by princes and princesses, using the veil, who have forgotten that they are also "All That Is". This new feeling of unconditional love, is so important that all princes and princesses must experience it before they can go "back" meeting the "new" essence of "All That Is". "All That Is" must really "think" about whether there are newer forms of love that still need to be created in future experiences!

You may have heard that "All That Is" is always the same. If this were the case, life would be without meaning. There are some who believe that life is "pointless".

If "All That Is" exists, development through creation and experiences is inevitable! An eternal evolving and growing awareness.

When you have digested the previous two stories and combined them with the first information about consciousness, I hope you have been able to get a bigger picture of what it is we, as humanity, are doing. I hope as well that you have extended your concept of yourself.

When I saw this picture, I felt both bigger, by having this importance, and humble for the role that I, as a creature of "All That Is", am playing. It is strange to turn from believing that I am only human, to know that I am also a human. Implied, that I am "All That Is", and even "All That Is" first and foremost.

For thorough study

- How would you define your relationship with "All That Is"?

- How would you define your surroundings relationship to "All That Is"?

- Is your definition influenced by your surroundings, or based on your own experiences?

- Are you "All That Is"?

Your growing understanding of your-self

Let's say that you, at some point in your life, have a specific pre-understanding of what "All That Is" is, and that you set out to find this "All That Is" somewhere out there in your future. Perhaps you make a large sign that describes this "All That Is" and place it in front of you, so you can always see what you're looking for. The following text is perhaps better understood if you compare it with the next illustration.

Now, when you move up your lifeline, you can be pretty sure to find "your" "All That Is", and you are maybe even happy for what you have found. But maybe the sign that you keep in front of you prevents you from seeing a new and larger picture of what "All That Is" is, as you get a greater insight. Perhaps your inner image of "All That Is" is changing, as you change and develop.

If you are able to see new points as you develop in your life, you may be able to take a new aim at a new point which is located higher up, meaning higher understanding, than the first one. You have become better qualified to judge as your wisdom grows. Let's say that you continue to grow and that the objective which you call "All That Is" also constantly changes. "All That Is" becomes more and more, or better that you "see" more and more, as you become more and more.

Maybe "All That Is" continues to grow, and maybe you will find that "All That Is" does not exist. Not in a way that you can understand in any way. The fact that "All That Is" is infinite really means that "All That Is" has no end, that "All That Is" is an infinite story! You might find out that you, and "All That Is", continue to grow indefinitely.

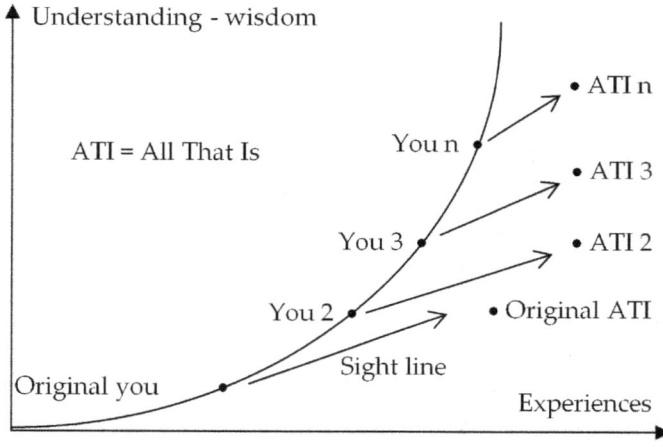

On the small graph above your development "starts" on the left-hand side and follows the curved line. The small "n" at the top, just tells you that the numbers will continue. I have made the curve become increasingly steep in order to show you that your development accelerates. The more wisdom you get, the better you will be able to grasp a larger and larger part of what "All That Is" is. Note that it is the human understanding of "All That Is" that we are talking about. Also, remember that "All That Is" learns through you and therefore, will grow with the wisdom that you acquire through your experiences.

For thorough study

• Can you remember any times when your concept of "All That Is" has changed?

The person and the observer

Until now, I have not been talking about what we call the person or human identity, but we can perhaps best describe it as the parts of a human being that are neithert the observer nor the physical body. A part of the human identity is the distracting thoughts and feelings that we were talking about at the start of this book. I will touch on how human identity is generated, but first I must answer the question: What is the reason for the observer to withdraw and leave the person in charge?

The observer has no need to prove itself, so it is the one that shouts the loudest that gets the word, and it is human identity! I would suggest that you see human identity at this stage as a small child, who has just started to learn every-thing about themselves and life. Look at it as a parent looks at its small child. It is also the observer's love for the timid human identity and his "right to choose", which leads the observer to keep a low profile. It is also called "the free will". By allowing the human identity to choose, we will get more experiences, as selected from a limited overview and from the feelings and de-sires that the person has.

For thorough study

- When you think of your life, are there any events that can have been started by the observer?

How the human identity is constructed

There are a few things that I have to mention briefly, and then I will elaborate later. As you know, we have, under normal circumstances, these senses: vision, hearing, taste, smell and touch. Now I will describe something that most people don't think of.

You've probably experienced, when entering a room, a sudden feeling that you did not have just before you entered. Let us imagine that the room is empty. You may not be able to define this feeling, but it might be unpleasant. Suddenly, you feel uncomfortable. What is actually happening here? How is it that you come into a room, feeling something that you did not feel a few seconds before? In the same way that, with sight, you can see what is in the room, you are able to feel the feelings that others have had in this room. You, therefore, have a real sense that senses feelings. You may have always thought that they were your feelings, and have not even considered whether they were the feelings of others. It is not a part of Western culture to feel emotions, but only to have them, so we are not aware of the possibility. It was a great experience for me, because I suddenly, for the first time understood that this was what happened to me.

The same applies to physical pain and thoughts.

If I feel pain, I become aware of whether it really is a signal from my body or someone else's pain that I feel. If some thoughts are popping up, which I do not immediately understand or can identify with, I also examine them closer. It is therefore a real possibility that many of your feelings, pain and thoughts do not belong to you.

You can now see that much of what we experience as our own, are really other people's feelings, pain and thoughts. We just take it for granted that they are our own. Next time you might feel that you need to take a few pills for headaches, you may ask whether it is actually your own headache. I usually remove these headaches by stroking both hands over my head from the forehead to the neck. Perhaps this should be done a few times and with the awareness that "now the pain has disappeared". By deliberately letting go of thoughts and emotions that are not yours, they may also disappear. See them not as something wrong; they just came past and you sensed them, and then you commanded them to leave you. It is like the smell of newly baked bread that sweeps your nose and continues on.

Now let's get started talking about human identity. The building up of the human identity starts in the mother's womb. The foetus is affected by its mother's thoughts, feelings and her body chemistry, both the signal substances in the blood and what she ingests. The embryo, at a time, will pick up sounds, including voices.

The researchers say that the body produces certain hormones, neuropeptides* that have to do with emotions. For every emotion, there is a specific peptide. This means that when the mother, for example, feels anger, a specific peptide is produced in her brain, which is then sent with the blood out of the whole body. I will elaborate on this later.

These are some of the reasons that children, in addition to the genetic heritage also "inherit" many of the parents' emotional patterns and opinions. They take them as their own.

As I said earlier, after the physical birth, the aspect of "All That Is" continues to build layer upon layer of things it gathers within the illusion by using other's opinions, allegations and views on itself and its own experiences and reflections and thereby building a human identity, and it now believes that this is what it is. To better understand what is happening, we can let the person have both a physical body, a body of thought (mental) and an emotional body. It is now these three that are constituting the human identity.

Imagine that the newborn child is called the master builder, and this master builder starts to build his house (human identity, etc.) out of the materials that it finds around itself. During life, the materials can be swapped if the master builder no longer feels that it belongs to the house. It is, however, not likely for most humans, to question whether these materials should be there or not. No matter how big the house becomes, the master builder remains the same, but with experiences from the collected materials. Here I must clarify that the materials are "tools" that provide experiences and, in the end, wisdom which becomes what changed "All That Is" from what it was yesterday to what it is today. At the same time, you can say that the core of "All That Is" does not change, just like the master builder does not change. An example of a tool can be an experience that you have in meeting another person who teaches you something about yourself. For example, you can learn that you are a really good in feeling into what this person needs, and you intuitively come up with a proposal for the person so that it corresponds with what he or she needs in his or her life. The tool, here, is meeting.

Now you might think that you have often

wished that your life was different, so as to remove some of the building materials in your house. Here you must bear in mind that you may have wanted changes, but not really believed you had the builder's power to change anything.

Now you can probably see that it really can be hard work to go through all these layers picked up through your life. The sooner you choose to define who you want to be, the easier it is. When you know what you have "picked up", you can choose from this and build your "house" as you, for this moment, want it to look like. You now live in the present moment creating your house from second to second, and therefore, you are always the one you want to be. You are authentic.

It is, in other words, where you take responsibility for your own life. There is really no other who could create it, no matter how much we blame the world around us for the things we experience in our lives.

Human identity is the tool with which the aspect or the observer acts in the world. The human identity is largely allowed to "live" on its own. It is the observer's wish that it is the person's feeling of being and longing for unity with "All That Is" that leads the human identity to look inward in "himself" to find its way to the observer and, ultimately, "All That Is". The human identity is a part of you, as long as you are on Earth. It is through the human identity that you will show yourself to the world.

When you start to look "inwards" to find yourself, the observer will be meeting you and when the observer begins a "push" to get out into the world, you may experience a fight for which part of "you" should be in command: you or the human identity! It is a natural part of the process, and I will return to this later.

For thorough study

- Do you have examples of how you have used your sense of feeling, either consciousness or unconsciousness?

- You may also have examples of thoughts that have been alien to you.

- Have you at one point felt other people's pain, but believed that it was your own?

The mass consciousness

As mentioned earlier, you can sense other people's thoughts, feelings and pain. Imagine that people's opinions, morals and beliefs are "hanging" around you as well. This is called mass awareness. In fact, it is also called "everyone". Here is also everything that "we" define as right and wrong, and, for example, what is healthy and unhealthy to eat. Here we could continue to give examples endlessly.

It is understandable that it is difficult to be "oneself" in such a world. This is really about feeling inside what is true for oneself and not feel OUTSIDE of what others think is right. Mass consciousness is the biggest barrier you have to find "yourself". In the beginning, it is difficult to continually be aware of feeling as yourself, but gradually it becomes something very natural. Over time, you will get a greater awareness of what is really you.

For thorough study

• Find examples of how mass consciousness affects your life.

• How does mass consciousness generally influence people's lives, their goals in life and their own development?

- What do you think mass consciousness is?

- Where does the mass consciousness come from and why is it here?

- Why is it important to have a mass conscious-ness?

- Do you know or have you heard about some-one who has chosen not to be influenced by mass consciousness?

To live outside the mass consciousness

To avoid being railroaded by mass consciousness, you first need to know what is you. You live in mass consciousness as a human identity and "above" this human identity is your real, immortal, I, which we also call the observer. Human identity is a necessary tool for you so you can interact with the outside world and mass consciousness. This is why you have taken physical form, so there is not something "wrong" in human identity and mass consciousness.

You can come to live **with** mass consciousness without living **in** it. Again, I must point out that the mass consciousness is not out to gobble you up; it is just the "soup" that the physical world works with. When you find out what that is, you have incredible opportunities and reserves to experience and do what you really feel.

I will now continue to talk a little about how mass consciousness effects and controls us.

For thorough study

- Try to find ways to live with mass consciousness on the basis of the examples found in the previous chapter.

Food

What is healthy or unhealthy to eat? This question may actually not be asked when it comes to what your body needs at the moment. You must therefore feel what your body needs. It is not what the human identity and the mass consciousness fancy, but what YOU feel that you really want. You can therefore still choose what you like, but the choice should just come from a deeper, inner desire, namely the body's needs. This may require much attention in the beginning. You can, of course, also choose to eat something, just to get the experience. If "All That Is" wants to experience yet another piece of pie, then that is just fine! However, there should be no guilt involved.

It is important what approach you have for the food you eat. If you feel bad and think that you eat unhealthily when you take a big piece of pie, you just feed your guilty conscience, but if you just enjoy it without condemnation, it is just another experience in the series of experiences which your life consists of. You have not sinned. SIN does not exist with "All That Is", only in humans just as "All That Is" does not judge. Why would "All That Is" judge his own desire to experience and create?

Think also of how much we try to control our bodies. Just look at how we try to control the body's nutritional needs by using more or less fixed dining times. We tell our bodies when they should take nutrition and fill them up. It should be the other way around! It must surely be the body that tells US when it needs fuel! "Yes but I will feel hungry just before supper time!" Of course, you yourself have programmed the body for this and then there is also the feeling of hunger from the mass consciousness that affects you.

I will give you an extreme example from my own life. On several occasions I heard about people who lived without eating, but gained energy from sunlight and only drank water and perhaps fruit juice. When I heard it from a reliable source, I decided to test this, not least in light of the fact that mass consciousness says we need food to survive and the right nutrients in order not to be sick. It was an important step for me on the road to reduce the influence of mass consciousness on my life.

It went well in the first three months, so I had proven to myself that it could be done. I had a minor weight loss but got more energy and also much more time since I did not have to buy, cook, eat or clean up afterwards, and I was not plagued by the laziness that comes after a meal.

When I look back, I can see why it was successful in the first three months, and why it was harder later on. I started in the spring when the weather was warmer, and the body did not require so much energy to maintain temperature and there were more and more bright hours. This also have an effect on mass consciousness. I did not make a gradual reduction of food intake but just stopped eating. I found it very difficult to drink "just" water, so I found a good syrup to mix in and some good juice. I began to drink more than I used to and found out that it was really good for the body.

I could tell you more, but I want to keep the story short, and bring it toward the early autumn when the temperature decreases as does the amount of light. I still did fine when I was at home and alone, but it was as if I was lacking energy and connection to Earth, as energy provider, when I was with many people. I attended the studies for a bachelor in Pedagogy at the time, and there was a clear difference between when I was in the midst of the many energies and when I was home. I brought some salad or fruit, and later I had to eat dinner on the days I had been at college.

The conclusion must be that I was influenced by mass consciousness and in close contact with the consciousness of my fellow students, and that I failed to keep myself completely outside of it. It also shows that sunlight is vital in order to keep the body functioning. I have, of course, learnt much, including that it is not necessary for me to eat a lot, and that I only had to eat when I feel it is necessary. It also depends on the energies around me. I also need to mention that it was boring not to eat, because the experience of dining is a big part of our lives and is used in many social contexts. At the time of writing, I eat what I like and when I feel like it, and eat in social contexts. I do not bother to walk down the aisles in a supermarket and am not bothered by the smell of food.

Now that you know that you can feel the emotions of others, you must also be aware of whether you are hungry, or if you feel someone's hunger. There is no reason why you eat for others, right?

For thorough study

- How is your relationship with food?

- What nourishes you most in your life?

- If your body should decide, would you eat differently?

- Do you consume something which you are addicted to, and how would you like your life to look according to this in, for example, two years?

- Why do you think that you ingest this?

Money

Let us look at money as energy. Just as money, energy is something we can use for many purposes. If we think of electricity and a lamp, the electrons will flow when you turn on the lamp. As the lamp uses energy it will draw new energy to itself. It can be seen as a vacuum, creating a vacuum that sucks more energy in. Try to look at cash in the same way.

Most people are extremely fixated by money (see the chapter entitled "Karma", about scarcity and abundance) and not least the phrase "what is saved is earned". This means that when you go to buy something you literally search for the "lowest prices". The quality issue will seldom come first, even if people are the more affluent. I am not talking about branded goods, just quality products. How much will you compromise on quality in order to pay a low price? This is about "just enough". Not just to pay less, but actually to get less. And the deeper meaning: how little do you want in your life?

Why not look at what you deserve in your life? When you use money and feel that you deserve what you buy (no comforting yourself), there will naturally be more resources for you. This does not mean that you simply must use all your money; this is about wisdom and insight.

Let me use petrol as an example. People are incredibly focused on petrol prices. How long a distance can you actually drive using the small amount of extra petrol you are able to buy? Alternatively, you may buy a large ice cream for the money you had saved... and you could have bought that ice cream anyway. Look at it in perspective! I hope you can feel I am smiling, for this is not criticism, just a "wake up."

Is there no money in your life? Is there only just enough to get by... or less? Has the cash flow stopped? When you stop spending money, the flow of money to you will stop. You must get the money to flow again. It is of course difficult to begin to use money which we do not have, but this is also about your approach to spending money.

For thorough study

- How do you see an item's price/quality ratio?

- What is your expectation for the ongoing disposal of resources?

- What relation do your parents and friends have to money and does it look like your own relationship to money?

Addictions

Dependency can very briefly be described as something we do and are incapable of stopping. We are therefore, dependent on this, since we cannot control it.

When you read what follows, I would ask you to have the mass consciousness's impact on you, in mind. "Is it really me who is dependent or is it the mass consciousness that affects me with the colossal sense of dependency it contains?"

When we talk about addiction, it is the human identity that is dependent. But what is it really that the human identity is dependent upon? Usually we think of various substances, but it can also be circumstances, actions and emotions that control us. They control us for the simple reason that we do not control them.

As I previously mentioned the brain produces certain hormones, neuropeptides*, that have to do with our emotions. These are sent through the blood stream to the whole body and affect the cells.

Imagine that you cannot only be dependent on substances that you take into your body but also substances that your body produces. I can mention that sex as one of the great examples. If we are dependent on one of these hormones, it means indirectly that we are dependent on the feelings that start the production of this specific neuropeptide. Since thoughts and emotions are closely interlinked, certain thoughts can indirectly lead to a kick which we can be addicted to.

Also, the body's cells can become addicted to certain substances. It happens because they have points on the surface that are called receptors* which do not receive stimuli in the form of signal substances or nourished. The cells then send a message to the brain to produce the desired substances. I will tell you how the cells work in the next chapter, about the body's decomposition.

Can you see where this is leading? By getting track of thoughts and emotions, you are calming down the body's chemistry so it comes into balance. This means the opposite too, that thoughts and emotions can lead to imbalances in the body's chemistry which, in turn, can lead to physical illness. I claim that by far the largest cause of all diseases in the body are imbalances in the human identity, including emotions, thoughts and the things that we pick up from others. The body only shows that there is something wrong. Note that when an imbalance is reflected in the physical body, it may have been there a long time, but on a non-physical level. For example, the emotions which I earlier called the emotional body or critical thoughts in the mental body.

In order to come into balance the cause must be found and obviously it does not exist in the physical. Perhaps the reason can be inferred from the physical, but the stabilising work must be carried out on other planes. One can work with balancing on multiple planes at the same time, but only symptomatic treatment of the body can remove the cause. It is not always that the symptoms in the body disappear when the cause is removed, so it is okay to work on the physical also, as long as we are aware that it is not here the actual work is performed. We can compare this with a bike tyre that is punctured by a nail. The reason is the nail, which in this case is invisible, but noteable. The procedure is: 1) feel to find the nail (the reason for the imbalance), 2) remove the nail (rebalancing), 3) seal the hole in the tyre (physical treatment) and 4) pump air in the tyre (get energy back in your life).

You do not need to know the exact cause of a symptom to cure yourself. It may be that the original reason lies far back in your life and that you therefore, under normal circumstances, are not able to find it. It may also be that there have been many similar, recurring reasons and it would be practically impossible to work through them all. We will cover this later. See the story about a cake box at the end of the chapter "Clear up".

For thorough study

- What substances, events, thoughts, emotions, feelings and so on, do you think you are addicted to?

- What or who has given you these?

- What will you lose if you got rid of the dependency?

- Which of the above topics is the easiest to liberate yourself from?

- Which topics can you overcome yourself and which do you think you need help with?

- Who can help you in this process?

Degeneration of the human body

I have mentioned the neuropeptides which are produced in the brain and are used to encode the body's cells. Each peptide has its own code and for the cell to get the peptide's information, it must have a receptor that fits the peptides' code as a key in a lock. If it fits, it can deliver its information or chemical substance.

A cell does not have an infinite number of recipients on the surface but there can be many different. When the cell divides, where the old dies and the new continues the work, it is determined how many and what types of recipients must be on the surface. Again this depends on what experience the old cell has had. If it was bombarded by many "I-am-not-good-enough" peptides, there will be more of these and less of the others.

Imagine that this feeling of not being good enough continues; there will be more and more recipients on the cell of this peptide and fewer of the other. The cell becomes more and more out of balance and may not receive other important information and perhaps not nutrients. Although the person now chooses to live differently, the cell has no opportunity to receive the substances that would make it a healthy cell. It is now imperative to turn this condition before the cell loses all its other receivers. In the longer term, the cell will determine that it no longer receives "I-am-not-good-enough" peptides and will in future generations replace the recipients with the others it needs, but it is a slow process.

If you want to keep your body healthy, it is necessary that you stay emotionally healthy and listen to the body's signals. Your body will tell you about imbalances and what it is missing.

This should give you hints about why, for example, diets usually only work for some time. It is primarily about what you feel and not what you eat. Some might say, "But if you eat a lot of fat and sugar it will settle as fat". The body will, under the right circumstances, discard the things which it cannot use, including fat, but there are feelings which, for example, make one want to protect oneself against the outside world, so the body creates an "armour of fat". The same applies if you feel that you cannot get enough so you must save for "bad times".

On the other hand, if you feel that you are comfortable with the world, you will always get what you need, and you will not even think whether you are too fat or not. Your emotions are in harmony and thus is your body.

In the chapter "Clear up", I will tell you how to communicate with your body's cells.

For thorough study

- Do you have emotions that burden your body?

- What caused these emotions?

- How can you bring more harmony into your life?

Feelings or emotions

In Denmark, we do not so much distinguish between emotions and feelings; we call them all feelings. Furthermore, we are talking about the sense of feeling although it is actually sensing touch, pressure and temperature we are talking about.

If we make a list of what we call emotions, with the "best" at the top and the "worst" at the bottom, for example, happiness and fear respctively, the top could be called feelings while the bottom is called emotions.

Feelings lifts you up while emotions drag you down. Feelings are deep, life, creation and action. Emotions are **re**acting. Feelings come "from the inside" while emotions are caused by something external. Feelings guide you while emotions control you. To make it even more complex, we can say that pure feelings are conscious "thoughts" or a "thought language", whereas emotions are reactions that act as a distracting noise to conscious thoughts.

In "reality" there is only one sense, the base feeling, love or peace, which is really "just" "All That Is's" sense of pure being or existing and that, in turn, is the total acceptance of all. This total acceptance is the knowing that everything is as it should be; that everything is perfect.

Of course, we must keep in mind that feelings are not good or bad, but in the human world all are made up of good and bad. This is primarily done so that we must learn to choose. Only by making conscious choices, can you determine your life, otherwise it is more external circumstances and your unconscious reactions which form your life. When we have learned to make conscious choices, we must learn to look deeper and discover that an immediate bad choice can be the choice that ultimately gives the "best" outcome. This exercise is about empathy. Therefore, to delve into what to choose instead of thinking and assessing what is best.

For thorough study

- Make a list of emotions and feelings, respectively, that you know.
- Then try to give them grades detailing how much influence they have on your life.

From a thought world to a feel world

In the chapter, "How human identity is built", I let the person consist of a physical body and a human identity that again consists of a body of thought (mental) and a feeling body (emotional).

Thoughts consist of words. Language consists of words. The language is limited both in expression and speed. There are limits to what can be expressed with words and although an idea is formed fast, they are still limited to how fast we can think. It takes time to think. We have the phrase "not to be able to put words to feelings". It shows both that feelings come before the thoughts, although thoughts can lead to feelings and that there are more feelings than words can describe.

By going from a thought-language to a feel-language as an inner dialogue, we can come up with solutions much faster and more accurately. Here, of course, it is not that we are controlled by emotions, which corresponds to what we previously described, but just a feel process instead of a thought process.

We can say that feelings have a wider spectrum than thoughts and are faster. Feeling is a higher conscious tool: conscious expression.

Here I can add that what we know as telepathy, that is communication by thoughts, would be more effective if we communicated with feelings. It does not take "time" to transfer "messages" and the communication is much more nuanced. I am not saying that it is wrong to think, just that there is something which is more efficient both in terms of speed and depth. See the end of the chapter "Consciousness", where I tell that thought is not the same as consciousness.

For thorough study

- Find examples from your life where you have noticed that your intuition came up with a solution before your brain.

- Did the brain come up with a workable solution?

- Can you draw any conclusions from your experiences?

The Brain

When the mind can no longer keep pace with our ever-accelerated lifestyles, it is necessary for our true feelings to take over most of the work. We simply cannot think fast enough to come up with the solutions we seek and take the decisions which we expect. Instead, let the "heart" feel what is the best choice for you, out of the endless possibilities that are at your disposal. There are no good and bad choices, there are just choices. For this to happen for all, we must go out of our minds, so to speak.

Let the brain and mind take care of the tasks they are meant to: your physical sensory system, the basic bodily functions, storage of information, automated tasks, and maintenance. The question is whether you can let go and show your body so much confidence that it can operate as intended. Human identity must no longer play the omniscience, but have the courage to leave the body and operate according to the specifications given to it when it was created.

When the workload of the brain is reduced dramatically, it opens up the possibility for the soul or the observer to communicate "wider" and more noise-free with our (nervous) system.

We have, from various sources, been told that the soul or the observer connects itself to the body through the brain. When our reality is created in the brain, it is convenient that the consciousness has direct contact with those areas of the brain involved in our perception of reality. That awareness connected to the brain, however, is not the whole truth. Each cell in the body contains a DNA code* which is the recipe of the entire human body. It is in this network that the communication between the consciousness and the body takes place. Quantum physics researchers have found that the space within each atom, between the nucleus and the electrons, is not empty, but consists of "consciousness". However, it is not the divine consciousness they have found, but possibilities and precursors into opportunities to be created by our consciousness. In other words, the body "swims" in these opportunities and the physical experiences we have are only an infinitely small part of each of us. Furthermore, the air we breathe is also made up of molecules which, in turn, consist of atoms. Therefore, it is not only "internal" but also external where we are swimming in this sea of possibilities.

For thorough study

- What meaning do the following concepts have for you: Consciousness, mind, brain, thoughts, human identity, memory?

From sensing feelings to knowingness

We have talked about using the sense of feeling instead of thought to determine what choices we want to make. You can put this "feeling into" a step further. Namely, by using your total awareness to gain certainty about beneficial choices or responses. I must once again mention that there is no right or wrong, but since you, the observer, have some demands about life, is it here the certainty comes in telling what choices and truths that are desirable to follow. Here it is not a vague feeling. You simply KNOW what to do. Imagine a blind person who must feel their way through a furnished and unknown room. Suddenly, this person is faced with the ability to know where all the furniture in the room is and thereby form an inner picture of the room. The blind person has not gained physical vision, but a deep understanding of how life looks like. And remember that sight can deceive.

We have now moved from being controlled by emotions to using the intellect, that is the thought to devise solutions, continuing to feel and finally to end up by the certainty that this is THE CHOICE.

For thorough study

- Try to find moments in your life where you, without the shadow of a doubt, have known how to act or what would happen in the next moment.

- Can you draw any conclusions out of your experiences?

Male and female

Men and women, male and female. At the beginning of the book, I was talking about the body without going into what sex it was. As a starting point, there are two genders, masculine and feminine. This applies to the majority of all life on Earth. Perhaps a signal to people that they cannot survive alone, and that we somehow belong together, that we are different and yet the same.

We are born as either a girl or a boy and identified as having this specific gender. As I was talking about earlier, we have a body, but we are not the body. Therefore, we can say that we have a gender, but not that we are a gender. For my part, I have a male body, but my real me, let's just stick to calling this me the observer, is not a man. As we came up with earlier, we are pure consciousness and consciousness, the observer cannot have a specific gender. The princesses and princes, as I have previously mentioned in a metaphor, are only used to make the story simpler. The souls, as little princesses and princes represent, do not have a gender. You will meet, or perhaps will have met, someone who talks about balancing the feminine and masculine. These two aspects dominate much of what is happening on the Earth. We can be more or less dominated by these aspects, and this is usually reinforced through our belief that we are either a woman or a man. Many suppress the opposite aspect in order not to risk being taken for something which they are not. Some have recognised that this gives an imbalance and are therefore working to bring this back into balance. The masculine and the feminine is part of the duality*, this dualism that exists in everything that is happening on our planet. Your real I, exists "beyond" this duality. You are neither the masculine nor the feminine and not a balanced creature with two sexes, but rather an asexual creature. To use the term creature, is disingenuous, since you are pure consciousness. It is hard to imagine that we are something as physically indeterminate as consciousness and not a physical thing.

Balance

I will now talk a little about balance and combining energies. I am going through some examples to bring you closer to the truth about balance. When we think that something is in balance, we usually imagine that we are in the middle and not at one or the other side and that there is equality.

There is much talk of balancing the feminine and the masculine energies as mentioned above. Imagine that you have two identical bottles in which we have our energies, one for feminine energy and one for masculine energy. If the two bottles contain the same amount, we can say that we are in balance. In reality, the energy is not in bottles of course, but they are not separate with the feminine and masculine energies on one side or the other. This is not correct to show it. Imagine that you have two pots of paint, a red and a blue and you mix them in a bigger pot. When you stir, in the beginning, you will see a spiral of red and blue paint. When you have stirred for some time, you get a violet paint. Each of the red particles in the paint is now separated from each other by the blue, and all the particles are also evenly spread within the mixture. If you imagine that you mix the two energies, they will interfere as paint, only with the difference that all the red energy still sticks together, and the same applies to the blue. The energies are still mixed, so it looks like a violet energy, but they retain their original affiliations, like two pieces of yarn entangled.

From balance to harmony

We live in a world of contradictions, in a world of dualities, where we believe that everything must have its counterpart. Good and bad, light and dark. There must always be a balance if things have to be optimal, you might say. If we speak of harmony instead, we will get a far better expression of sheer natural condition. Harmony has no need for opposing forces; harmony is in balance with itself. Balance in unity, not in duality.

Think of how much easier life would be if you did not constantly have to keep balance on the narrow road of life, but could just glide in the direction you choose.

For thorough study

- What would you do if you were not bound by having to act as a specific gender?
- Find examples of what you have to work on in order to find balance in your life.
- How will your life look when it is in harmony?

Clean up

Now that we have talked a great deal about how we became who we are and why the world is as it is, is it easier to get started with the cleaning up process and find out what it is we want in our lives.

In the chapter "Dependency", I claim that the vast majority of all diseases in the body are caused by imbalances and too much disharmony in the human identity, including emotions, thoughts and the things that attach themselves to us from others. The body shows physically that something is wrong. Note that when a disharmony is reflected in the physical body, it may have been there a long time, but on a non-physical level, as I have mentioned earlier.

You might say that a broken arm is a purely physical injury or imbalance in this language. You have undoubtedly been in situations where you could easily have broken an arm, but where it did not happen. The reason you broke the arm this time may be because you were not aware because you thought of a problem or there was something that worried you. Therefore, an imbalance in your emotions caused this change in your life. You can also get an "aha" experience because of the broken arm, a revelation that tells you that you need to do things differently in your life by using the other hand. Perhaps it is a way to get you to calm down and get a better overview of what happens in your life. Or you may get the opportunity to meet a person who can help you make changes in your life. So why not say, "Yes I have a broken arm! What options have I given myself to evolve?" It is not something external that made you break your arm, and the way you react to it is not the punishment of "All That Is"!

It is important always to ask why we are in a given situation. Maybe the whole situation is laid out in a certain way so you may learn something from it. It may also be that your way of solving a problem may serve as a model for another. You do not have a problem; you have just been given a chance, with this tool quite literally, to show how it can be solved.

Communicating with the cells in your body

In the chapter "Dependency", we talked about how the body's cells can lose the ability to receive things from the outside. I would like to tell you a little more about the cells.

I would ask you to see the body as a collection of cells that work and communicate among themselves, and not as one thing built up of bones, flesh and organs. An organ is a collection of cells with the same task or, in the case of the liver,

500-600 tasks. It is not the body that makes the work; it is the cells.

Researchers tell us that every cell in the body contains the code for how the entire body is constructed. They talk about the DNA strand. Now imagine that each cell has a consciousness and that this consciousness is working together in a common body consciousness that has knowledge of the code in the DNA string. Therefore, every cell and its function and status is accounted for. We can say that every cell is intelligent, and they all work together in a higher intelligence. It sounds very logical. The cells cannot just work for themselves, but must necessarily interact and be aware that this interaction may change at any moment.

This also means that it is the cells, or more precisely the body consciousness, that best knows how the body works. Only a few researcher has this knowledge. Therefore, it must also seem strange to the cells that you, via researchers and other clever people, are trying to tell the body how it should work and what it needs. However, since you are the boss, the cells shrug their "shoulders" and say, "OK, you're the boss, if you want to play that way and have these experiences, then it is fine with us."

In fact, it should be the other way around. It should be you who should listen to your body when it tells you what it needs!

Even your body tells you that it needs certain building blocks, and when they no longer are needed. Why take vitamin pills throughout the year if it is only necessary for the cells to obtain this subsidy in one month a year and maybe even in varying doses within this period?

When we want to create balance or rather harmony in our body, it is obvious to communicate this wish to the cells via the body consciousness. After all, it is the cells that must perform the stabilising work. There will always be completely healthy cells in your body. Instruct those cells to send information about how they are built and ask the unbalanced cells to use this information in their own maintenance work. Do not make this process complicated with rituals, just finish this short communication with an underlying knowledge that the cells know what to do. Then bless the cells. It all takes under a minute. If you feel that you must see a doctor, you may of course do so, this may be the solution, but you must not hand your responsibility for your body over to the doctor. This is the responsibility you took upon yourself when you decided to get the body.

The stones in the cake box

I will conclude this chapter with something that my "higher" self brought forward before a meditation evening with some acquaintances. Note that I refer to myself in the plural. It really requires a longer explanation, but in short, it is that we are all connected and some are joining to convey some messages:

"Now we say something that you may not like to hear. If you want to see who you really are in this moment, you will need to remove all the shadows from the past that bind you to it. Yes, we know that you say it is the past that has made you into the you that you are, but think of all the threads that bind you to the things that you thought you were, but have really picked up from others. Just think of the times when you have seen one of your parents in yourself and even acted on or used a specific phrase of theirs. Release all this and locate the core, essence and wisdom.

"Let us paint a small picture that might make it easier for you to understand what we mean. Imagine that you are a child. Occasionally, you pick up stones, sometimes because of their colour, other times because of their shape or surface. You put the stones in your pocket and when you come home, you put them in a cake box with all the other stones that you have picked up on earlier excursions in your young life. Then one day when you have grown older, you find the cake box hidden with your old stuff. It has not been opened for a long time, and it is old, rusty and hard to open. When you finally get the lid up, you look at all the stones and smile. You take them up one after another and look and feel them again. You can recognise some of them. Some make you remember events, but mostly you can no longer understand why you picked them up.

"You now have two piles of stones on the table. One pile, the largest, contains the stones that you immediately want to throw out, while the smaller pile contains the stones which bring back memories. You sit for a while and think about why you should keep the stones in the small pile. You will probably not even look at them again. You decide to store all your memories in your heart and drop all ties to the stories because they are not the memories.

"Now would be a good time for you to let go of all your imaginary stones. You do not have to look in your cake box and pick up every single stone to find out which you want to keep. You can just say to yourself that you let go of all the ties and only retain the wisdom in your heart. And do not be afraid that your heart will be too small to hold them all; it will simply grow larger so that they can all be there."

For thorough study

- Can you find the wisdom and learning from some events in your life that you may define as bad or unpleasant?

- Do you have the courage to cut all the ties that prevent you from living the life you want?

Karma

You may have heard about the concept of karma, but depending on who you ask, you get different answers on what it means. The Western world's understanding of karma is, in short, that what you do to another you must experience yourself. It is also what is called cause and effect. It happens so you can get the full understanding and wisdom of what an event contains. I would like to tell you what my "higher" self relayed to me about karma with the title "scarcity, suffering, abundance and joy":

"Most people in the world today are not willing to accept the fact that the treadmills they call their lives are worn out and the wheels their lives are running on, no longer run as evenly and smoothly, but actually are very much in need of some oil. They are creaking, and the sound is annoying for everyone in and around his or her life. The noise should waken them, so they can get an overview of their lives and consider the possibility of replacing the whole vehicle. Not that they should replace the body, but radically change the way they live."

"The most obvious thing to do is to consider a whole new way of thinking. There must necessarily be a very different way to connect to the real self, i.e. the soul. By this, we mean that the best way to do this is by connecting to the higher self, to a degree, so that they are able to hear their own divine voice telling them what their goals and purposes in life are about."

"The first step is to get rid of old beliefs around scarcity and suffering and instead greet a life of abundance and joy."

Scarcity, "I believe that there is not enough for all. I think that you have to collect as much as possible for yourself, just to be sure to survive. This is leading to the belief that you do not have enough and thus initiates a vicious circle. But why would a creator, God or otherwise, create surroundings for his children, where there are not enough necessities for them to get through life with the greatest possible livelihood?"

Suffering, "The idea of having to suffer as a punishment from a vindictive God can only be a human concept. How can a small creature such as man see itself as being able to offend such a mighty creator? It is in a way understandable that people give their God human qualities. Moreover, a God which they themselves have created in their thoughts. Not to say that there is no God, but to say that what you call God is indefinable in human words and incredibly more than what you can imagine. So why should any creator, God or anything else create such bad conditions for its children, so they must suffer?

"You have not **created** the suffering to suffer,

but **chosen** it to experience the opposite of happiness. To get the full benefit of the experience, it makes no sense that you should be staying in suffering, surely! Make a new choice!"

Abundance, "We have a different definition of abundance than most people. Abundance is simply this: that in every given moment you have what you need. Not everything which you might like to have, but all that you need to implement what you have chosen to do. So if you know that you will always have what you need at any time your lives will be much more relaxed. Also, remember that perhaps there is not a parking space when you need one, because you have to park somewhere else for a reason that you might only realise later. Perhaps it is here that you meet a person who can play an important role in your life. There is always a reason for things to happen."

Joy, "Joy in life simply comes to you, when you chose to enjoy life. Do not expect to **get** joy in life, but know that you **have** joy in life. As we said, there is always a reason for things to happen. So if you pay attention to the small things that can lead to happiness in your lives and follow them, you will naturally get more joy."

Between the lines of what I've just said is actually the fact that you can consciously choose what you want in your life. It therein lies also that you can be opt out things in your life. You also choose how you look at your world. In the divine perspective, you cannot be punished through karma for something you do in your life, just as well as you will not be rewarded for "long and faithful service". Your actions can, of course be "seen" in your "colours" on the soul level, but there is no condemnation, just acceptance.

And finally: forget about fate. The concept does not exist. It is simply a way to evade responsibility for one's own life, and it is of the utmost necessity for your development, that you take responsibility for your life, then it will be built up by many more conscious choices, and you feel that you have an overview of what is happening.

For thorough study

- What does it mean to you to have the courage and the willingness to take responsibility for your own life?

- What does it mean for you to be responsible for your life – exactly?

The catalyst

I will briefly introduce you to the concept of the catalyst. A catalyst can be a substance that causes two other substances to react with each other faster than they would otherwise and without the catalyst itself is included in the outcome. Imagine that you can have the function of a catalyst in other people's lives. As you become more aware of who you are and what is happening around you, you can use your knowledge to help your fellow humans to get a greater understanding of their lives.

When you can emotionally stand outside and look at what is going on around you, without it "sticking" to you, you can have a much greater understanding of situations. You can use this understanding to determine whether the situation has something to do with you or whether you have just entered into these events. You may use your knowledge to help in a given situation. Just remember that your fellow human beings do not have this understanding, and you should therefore take this into account if you mingle. If it has nothing to do with you, you can either just give acceptance to what happens or be the catalyst that, with minimal effect, can change the situation. Sometimes it is best not to interfere because the parties necessarily should find a solution by themselves. If they do not solve the conflict by themselves, they might not get the "aha" experience that is necessary for their continued learning. Remember this!

Also, remember that a catalyst does not interfere in other people's lives to tell them how they should live! The catalyst teaches his or her wisdom through the example and gives people insight, if they ask for advice.

For thorough study

- Find examples where you have acted as a catalyst.

- Do you have examples of how others have been catalysts for you?

- Do you feel that you can be a catalyst for your fellow human beings and, if so, why?

Part 2: Illusions

Dimensions

We find it difficult to imagine a world that does not have three dimensions. How can a "room" have four dimensions? Or how would it be to live in a world with only two dimensions where there is no height? If you have no height, how can we see each other? A cell without height, may well not exist. No matter what you think of these cases, you have only your three dimensions to compare with, and since it is precisely the dimensions you are using as a base for your views, your 3D brain is unable to come up with something workable. You will need to rewrite these situations into a 3D model that your intellect can relate to.

Actually, we cannot talk of dimensions as spaces. Dimensions are more a way to perceive a state of existence. Not something static as there is always movement. By accepting that there is something that your intellect cannot understand, you come a long way from being able to access other dimensions. You have thus removed the biggest barrier to achieving being "out" of the physical dimension.

The following picture may give you a sense of how dimensions can be seen: imagine that each dimension is an orchestra with its own instruments and own musicians, but the sub-harmonics come from All That Is. This means that each orchestra plays its own unique music, but because of the divine sub-harmonics, All That Is is hearing all of the orchestras as one huge symphony orchestra where each tone from each instrument, played by each musician, is included as a unique part of the experience. This also provides a beautiful picture of how each of us, as the musicians we are in our lives, play each of our tones in God's great orchestra.

You may have noticed that if you have a glass of water with a straw in, and you look through the glass from the side, it seems that the piece of the straw above the water is not connected with the part under water. If you're looking down from above, you may see that the straw bends in the surface of the water. It is easier to see if the water is deeper, for example, if you are doing the experiment with a stick in a lake. If you must catch fish with a spear, you must first determine how much "wrong" you must aim to hit the fish. It also depends on the depth.

This is just one example which I use to show you that every time we are in one medium - in this case the air - and look at something in a different medium - the water - there will be a shift.

If you need to "look" from one dimension to another, which may also be considered as two media with different densities, such as water and air, you must use your consciousness. Here you need to find out which dimension you want to "look" at, and how much you should shift your aim. And again, the dimensions must not be seen as space.

Since we usually use our physical senses and our intellect to explore everything in our world, it is really a challenge to use consciousness instead. You might have to work for some time before you intuitively correct for this offset. You can compare it with the situation where you have to practice throwing a ball through a hole in a fence. Only when you intuitively know how hard you have to throw and at what angle, does it begin to be easy.

For thorough study

- Have you had any experiences you have not been able to explain to yourself with your intellect?

- What can it tell you?

Tiredness

I will briefly look into the concepts of being tired and sleepy, which is a little connected to the next section about dreams. I choose to give the two concepts different meaning. When you feel tired, you must rest and when you feel sleepy, you must sleep. Resting is not the same as sleeping, although you can rest while you sleep.

When you rest, you are relaxing the physical (body), intellectual (thoughts) and emotional (feelings). When you sleep, you give the soul a "recess" from the physical, where you as a soul can escape from the gravity of duality. You, as the soul, do not lose connection to the body, but you have probably had some experiences with sudden awakening and the feeling of not being you or yourself.

If you feel tired, you need to rest. This is about the body, thoughts, and feelings.

If you feel sleepy, you must sleep. This is the Soul's "time off" from the 3D world.

The body is designed to not need rest if it is not overloaded, so it is usually your mental and emotional "bodies" that you "wear out". This tells us that we put too much load on these bodies. Too much thinking, worrying and feeling in our reacting to the outer world.

The concept of the power nap describes how

you can take a short nap - for example, ten minutes - and subsequently have much energy. This tells us that even a short interruption of everyday life, can re-establish the energy supply from the planet to our own "internal" energy system. It also tells us that it is an illusion that we humans must sleep, on average, for eight hours a day, and preferably in one stretch to be what we call rested.

For thorough study

- How much sleep do you need to feel fresh and rested the next day?

- The need for sleep may vary through life. What can the need for sleep be dependant on?

- What drains your energy? It can be both something from the outside world and something from yourself.

Dreams

Dreams have always given rise to much specu-
lation and there have been many explanations
as to what this phenomenon really is, and what
good it does.

Dreams can be messages that can be understood
directly or experiences in other dimensions that
you can only take back to your waking understanding in a down-transformed* form. I talked
a little about this in the chapter "Dimensions",
where an experience in another dimension could
not be understood directly by the intellect. It
will therefore only be fragments, small pieces of
the entire episode that will come "back" to the
3D environment.

Try to inquire into these dreams just before you
completely wake up. It may give you a better
understanding. Maybe you will get an explanation of something in your life or a possible solution to a task you have been struggling with for
some time. The answer may turn up at a later
time, so do not expect an answer right away.

You may also inquire into the feelings you had
in the dream and maybe think about which of
those connections you had or have in your life.
It can point towards something that you have
to resolve in your life. It is also important to understand that the people that you know in your

waking life and who appear in dreams, can act as "tools" or messages to show you different feelings or behaviour patterns. You must not necessarily link these people to feelings and actions that appear in the dream. In other words, for example, you must not bear any grudges towards a person if this character has given you a specific feeling in the dream. One can say that it is more important to focus on the feeling than the situation and finally, the person. The person in the dream can also act as "mirror" showing how you are acting in your own life. In other words, you experience yourself, just from a different angle.

The reason you may not find the head and tail in some dreams can have the following explanation. As you become more and more aware of whom, or what, you really are, your human consciousness and your soul consciousness are melting more and more into one. Your consciousness is becoming one. The consciousness that experiencing something in other dimensions is the same that is active in your so-called waking state, but here it is just limited by the three-dimensional world if you use your mind. Therefore, your intellect does not quite comprehend the different events taking place in other dimensions. It tries to compare them with something it knows. Therefore, the many pieces will be put together into a chaotic dream. This is actually the biggest intellectual limitation, namely that it always goes to the past for answers. It lives in the past. This also means that you have to be "out of the mind" to be fully present in the now moment.

Another thing that happens when you sleep, and give the soul time off, is that you test various actions in other dimensions, in order to find the best action in your life on Earth. You go into a laboratory and test the various choices, and then you try to bring "back" the best in relation to what you want to achieve in your life. Imagine that you place the result in the soup of possibilities you always have "around" you. It will make it more likely that you choose this action, especially if you think about how you want to choose. You always have to FEEL for the choice, because you cannot THINK to get it from your energy field. Therefore, feel and act; do not think and act.

For thorough study

- Find episodes where you have felt what you should do without having thought of it first. We say that you act intuitively.

- It may be a good idea to make a dream diary. Later, when you read it again, you must be aware of the words and phrases you have used. Why did you use this exact phrase? Did you use words which you do not normally use?

Time

At one point, I asked myself, meaning my higher self, what I could say about the concept of time. This is my answer:

The experiment "to be outside of time":

"You have probably seen and felt that time passes faster or slower than you might expect of a given experience."

"We need to distinguish between two kinds of time, the time that we can see at our watches and the time that we feel. We cannot do much about the time on the clocks, but the time that you feel is much easier to work with. The time on our clocks is just ticking, second by second, no matter what we do. The "feeling time" is, however, a feeling of an event in progress."

"Imagine that you participate in an event, and you feel wonderful. A lot happens during the event, but when you look at your watch, you do understand that all this has happened in such a short time. The answer is that you have been in a state of pure pleasure in which you have created this "feeling time", or rather, you have experienced something outside the clock time.

"On the other hand, when you later look back at such an event, you may think that it had been going on for quite some "clock time". It is because you now set the amount/length of events equal to the clock time; the events "should" have taken in relation to the perception of the clock time you have. If a lot had happened, or it had a great impact on you, it should have taken a long "clock time".

"An example of how you work with the "feeling time": let us say that you are waiting for a bus. This waiting is bound to you "feeling" and you feel that time goes slowly because nothing happens in this period. If you, instead of waiting, just sit or stand in the present moment, you will move outside time and had just "been" instead of "doing" this waiting. You are actually an event instead of "doing" an event! This event is a part of you because you created it."

"Practice not to check the time using the devices you are carrying with you. You will quickly learn to feel what time it is, or better, when it is the right time. Do not become a slave of time. Thus, you have only 24 hours a day. You must not live in "time", but experience events! You must not "make" events, but be events. Please be aware that you have created the event to start with and what you create belongs to you."

As you may have noticed, the fact that you create the "feeling time" is mentioned several times. This means that this information is very important. It also tells you that you create your life and just as important that you must take responsibility for it! The talk of "clock time" and "feeling time" is merely to satisfy your intellect, thoughts and mind.

Past, present, future

When we talk about the present, we can really only talk about this moment, here and now, as it is here our consciousness is. It is not the whole day or "in this modern time". We can think of the past and imagine the future, but we only exist in the present moment.

Here you have another small story from my "higher self". It is called The Soup Pot.

"We will tell you what happens in what you call the future; it is connected with the past. Not to say that "the past" creates the future, but only that past choices have an influence on today's choices. Past energy interfering with the present energy and thus affecting the choices that are in "front" of you, meaning the choices that you are most likely to make. Imagine a big pot of soup already containing many ingredients, which have been added in the past which may, at any given time, give the soup its current taste, smell and texture. Unlike an ordinary soup, with your life's soup you can remove any ingredients that you no longer want to be part of the soup. Removing ingredients gives you, so to speak, space so that new, exciting things can be added to the soup.

"You are the creator of your life and are therefore, the only one that can actually change it. So simple, it can be said! And remember that you are a chef and not the soup!"

For thorough study

- Find moments in your life where your perception of time has been different than you expected.

- Can you draw any conclusions from your experiences?

Relationships

Generally the largest challenge in a relationship is to overcome the fear of being abandoned or to lose someone!

I have been asked and have also previously wondered, "why do you live alone? It does not appear that you are looking for a partner."

Many are looking outside themselves for what they feel they want or cannot live without, and that indicates that they are missing something; that they are not whole. We are looking for a partner with the qualities that we feel we do not have ourselves. This signal to your life is therefore, "I am not good in myself; I am missing something." This attitude is then expressed in your life, and you therefore, live a life where you are missing something.

We expect the outside world to supply the deficiencies and by living with a focus outside of ourselves in the eternal quest, we never find out who we really are and what we contain. We only know that we are missing something that others must give us. We must therefore go out and sell ourselves, prostitute ourselves to shop to get our needs covered. Even if we find a partner who matches the deficiencies, we are still only half a person. The rest exists in the other person. We, therefore, need to reclaim ownership of the other person to make demands on the abilities. This relationship can be described as a master-slave relationship or a relationship where we ourselves are the slave. One can, of course, also be dependent on having to be the master.

When you have found the partner who has everything you are missing, appreciate and admire, life is in the beginning all roses. But it is precisely the great dissimilarity which fascinates and will also be the glitch in the relationship in the long term. If we are able to share and integrate the differences equally, there is a great chance that the relationship will flourish.

I am looking inwards because I know that I contain much more than that I immediately am aware of. The more I examine inward, the more I come to know myself, and the more I feel whole.

If I must have a partner, it must necessarily be a "whole" person, so the relationship consists of two whole individuals rather than two "halves".

Since I am not looking for a partner because it is not necessary for me to find something I need outside myself, is it not likely that I will find a partner. This way, I create my own solitary life; not to be confused with loneliness.

For thorough study

- Can you recognise this quest for what we think is missing in our lives?

- What are you looking for?

- What is it that you admire in a person you look up to?

- What can you do to start the process of promoting these qualities to yourself?

Accept yourself as you are

You have probably experienced being in love and also loved that person's "faults," which just makes that person special. Do the same for yourself. Take time to be alone with yourself as your beloved is also yourself. Since we identify ourselves very much with our bodies, it is a good idea to start to love it. Indulge in it, give it attention, bless it as I previously talked about the body's cells. Show that you are grateful that you have it because you could not act on the physical level without it. I hope that you will be able to feel at one point that it loves you too. Remember that you are not your body. It is essentially an autonomous creature that you, as consciousness, have "borrowed" from Gaya, the diva of the Earth.

By accepting yourself with all your "flaws" and crazy whims and being able to laugh at your re-actions and "accidents", you make your life a fun play or a fun movie, rather than a drama or a tragedy.

Love yourself as the creature of "All That Is" that you are, and see yourself as a vital musician in the great orchestra of "All That Is". Without you, the music cannot be perfect, and "All That Is" is just perfect. This means that "All That Is" cannot exist without you and the music you play!

For thorough study

- Try to find some things in yourself that you could love in another person.

- What can you do to love and honour your body?

All is well

The heading "All is well" is some claim, but I will use it to provide you with a more relaxed view about what is happening around you. By understanding that there is always a reason for what happens or does NOT happen, you will get fewer of the "negative" emotions and thoughts that bring you out of balance and take your energy, to become indignant, feel that it is a shame, that something is not fair, that anyone should be punished, and so on. Expressed in popular terms, to see life around you as a large play, where most participants have forgotten that they are "only" playing and that they themselves have helped to write this play, you can more easily accept what is happening "out there", as acceptable actions, without immediately being able to see the point of them.

By just being the observer and not participating and being judgemental and to let your thoughts and emotions be in charge, you will see the meaning much more easily, perhaps not immediately, but at a later time. However, you cannot expect it to always make sense for you. It is not certain that you are included in a particular "play" and therefore, it is not played for you.

For thorough study

- If you knew that everything was as it should be, how would your life be?

- What things in your life would you change immediately?

- What things would you change in the longer term?

Conclusion

After reading this book, you may come to the conclusion that most of what I have written about, is an illusion. It is strange for me as well just to be able to write about something which does not exist, in reality, without being able to explain with words what reality really is.

I trust that you have trained your distinction ability, and your common sense has brought you to the end of the book. If you have been able to work with the points at the end of each chapter, I am sure you have come to know yourself better. It might have cost you "blood, sweat and tears", hopefully mostly the latter, but as with everything in life, we come out on the other side with a greater understanding of life and at the same time with a wisdom which we can choose to share with others on our way.

I remember how frustrated I was during much of the work I did while I attended the healer school. I had great opposition to many of the things that lay just below the surface of my awareness and should have also worked through the anger which arose when I blamed my surroundings for these things even though, deep down, I knew that I had only myself to thank.

I have been very open with you about different things from my own life, and I hope that you also will be open to those aspects of yourself as you meet and recognise them for what they are. It is important to stand by what you are and a necessity if you must stand as an authentic person to other people and other creatures and to meet them as equal members of this creation, which we call the world.

I hope that you can use the information and guidance which I have presented to you, and that you have become more convinced that you can choose how much of what you are experiencing should be allowed to fill your life. This applies to both outer and inner experiences and thoughts, feelings and emotions.

I could choose among much good advice, but I choose to give you this: be present in your own life and enjoy it, both when you are a player and when you are the audience.

Blessed be you for what you are!

THE END

I hope you have enjoyed the book and ask you to take a moment to make a short review on your favourite retailer website.

Thanks in advance, Erik Istrup

Part 3: Addendum

Meditation

Vipasana meditation technique

This is a very easy meditation technique called Vipasana. It is a rational method for purifying the mind of the mental factors that cause distress and pain. This simple technique does not invoke the help of a god, spirit or any other external power, but relies on our own efforts.

Find the link in the "References" section or search the internet for guidelines.

References

The references are both sources that have inspired me and sources which could be used to elaborate on some of the topics that I have mentioned.

Hudson, Geoffrey, "The Miracle of Birth - A Clairvoyant Study of Prenatal Life"
http://hpb.narod.ru/MiracleBirthGH.htm
- www.geoffreyhodson.com.

Lipton, Bruce H. (2005), "The Biology of Belief".
- www.brucelipton.com

Muhl, Lars, "The Law of Light - The Aramaic Mystery".
- www.larsmuhl.com/uk/index.html

Use the internet. There is a lot of "bad stuff" out there; it reflects the mass consciousness, but there is also very real and useful information. Perhaps it just what you are missing to get a new angle to make progress towards a greater understanding and awareness of the whole.

Double slit experiment: www.whatthebleep. com
Search on "Dr. Quantum" to see a video that describes the experiment. Scientists have proven that consciousness affects our world.

Vipasana meditation technique:
- www.vipassanadhura.com

About the Author

I was born in Lemvig, Denmark in 1961. I observed my first UFO in the 8th year in public school, at noon in a recess, so I always knew that there was something out there. I did, however, later receive another vision of what UFOs are, but it is outside this topic of this book.

I am a trained draftsman, technical assistant and electronic engineer, having completed my latest work as a technician in 2005 and obtained a Bachelor of Pedagogy degree in 2010.

In 2003, I started at the Healer School in Aabenraa, and completed level one in 2005, which was a major step towards a more metaphysical approach to life. During this period, I got in contact with several people, who were not in physical form, which gave me additional insights. As I got more confidence in my own abilities, I could gradually feed into information that could benefit me in my everyday life.

I feel that my life is currently pointing towards dissemination, information and guidance with "you are more than you think, see and experience" and I seek to do things in new ways.

- Erik Istrup

www.ingramcontent.com/pod-product-compliance
Lightning Source LLC
Chambersburg PA
CBHW061657120626
46550CB00003B/981